AF594500

UNITED STATES
Maria Koran and
John Willis
EYEDISCOVER

Go to **www.eyediscover.com** and enter this book's unique code.

BOOK CODE

**AVF62736**

**EYEDISCOVER** brings you optic readalongs that support active learning.

Published by AV2
276 5th Avenue, Suite 704 #917
New York, NY 10001
Website: www.eyediscover.com



Library of Congress Control Number: 2021937114

ISBN 978-1-7911-4208-7 (hardcover)

Printed in Guangzhou, China
1 2 3 4 5 6 7 8 9 0 25 24 23 22 21

042021
102120

Project Coordinator: John Willis
Designer: Mandy Christiansen

The publisher acknowledges Getty Images and Shutterstock as the primary image suppliers for this title.

EYEDISCOVER provides enriched content, optimized for tablet use, that supplements and complements this book. EYEDISCOVER books strive to create inspired learning and engage young minds in a total learning experience.

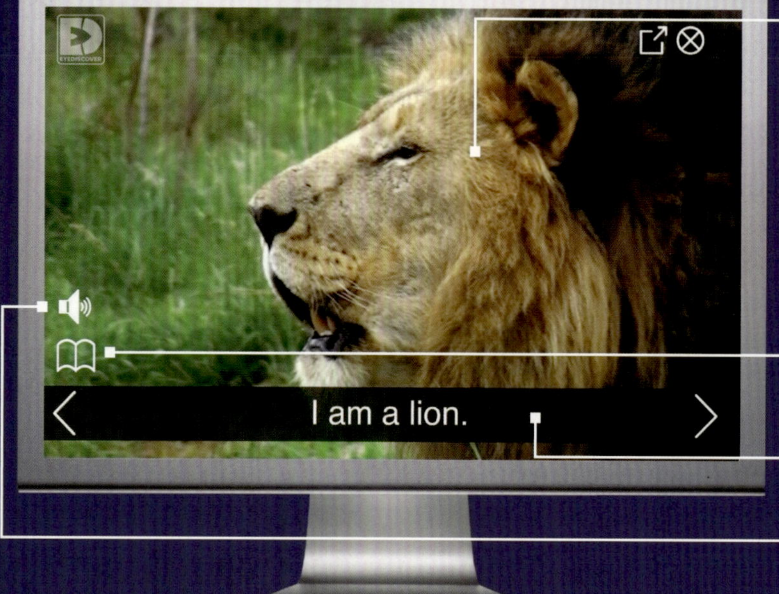


**Watch**
Video content brings each page to life.

**Browse**
Thumbnails make navigation simple.

**Read**
Follow along with text on the screen.

**Listen**
Hear each page read aloud.

## Your EYEDISCOVER Optic Readalongs come alive with...

**Audio**
Listen to the entire book read aloud.

**Video**
High resolution videos turn each spread into an optic readalong.

**OPTIMIZED FOR**

- ✓ TABLETS
- ✓ WHITEBOARDS
- ✓ COMPUTERS
- ✓ AND MUCH MORE!

# UNITED STATES

In this book, you will learn about

- what it is
- who lives there
- what it is known for

and much more!

The United States is a country in North America. It is next to both Canada and Mexico.

MULAN
PAN AIRLINES
JAL
JAPAN AIRLI
BE MORE CHILL
"AN EPIC, DAZZLING THRILL RIDE."
HAVE A REALLY GOOD TIME TONIGHT
PRETTY WOMAN
COME FROM AWAY
KING KONG
McDonald's Restaurant
EXPRESS
LAMAR
SONY
FDNY

The United States has many cities. More people live in New York City than in any other U.S. city.

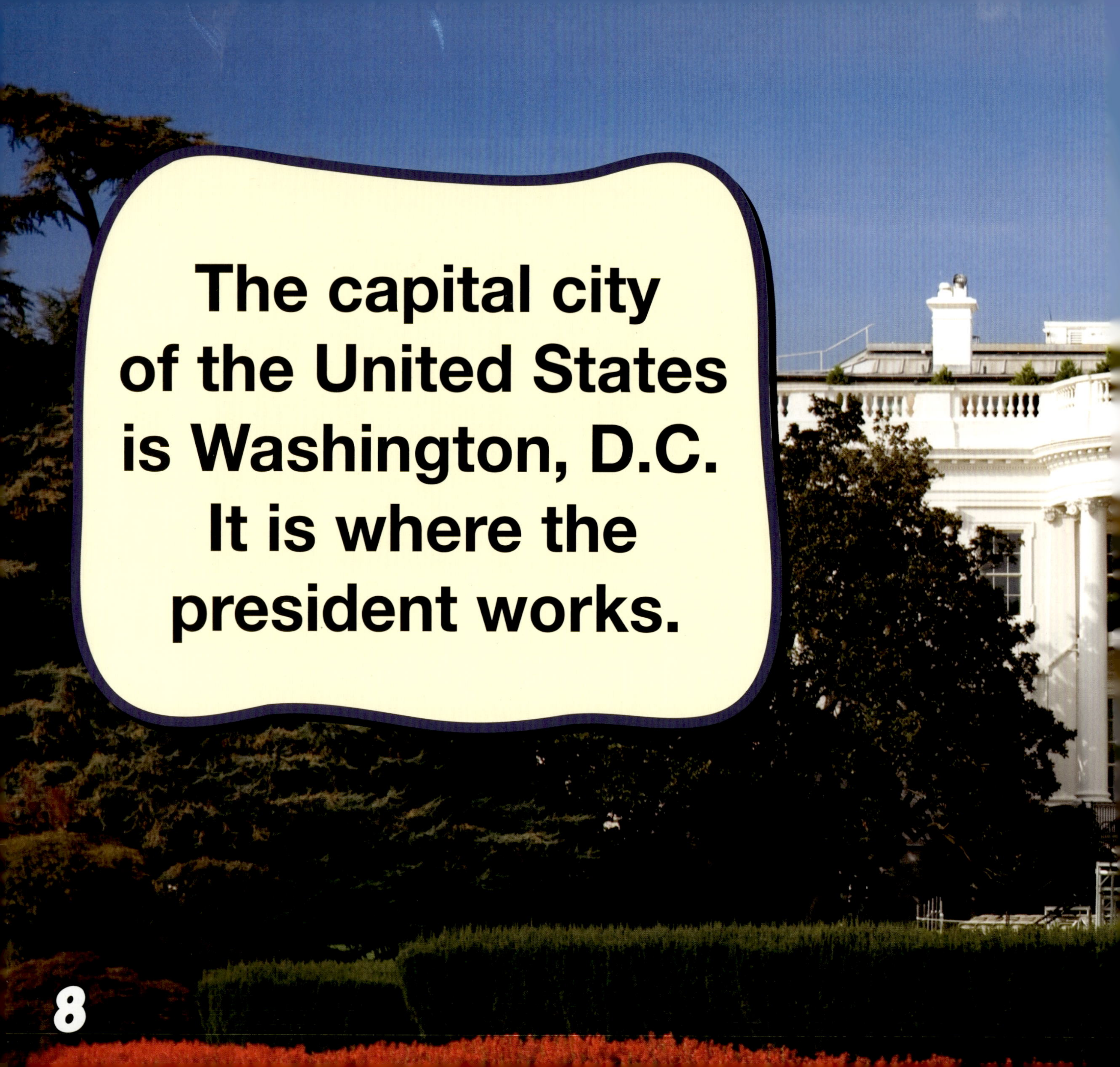

The capital city of the United States is Washington, D.C. It is where the president works.

There are 50 U.S. states. The country's flag has one star for each state.

California is the state with the most people. About 40 million people live there.

There are many symbols for the United States. The U.S. national mammal is the American bison.

America has a national bird, too. It is the bald eagle.

People visit many U.S. landmarks. The tallest mountain in the United States is called Denali.

The Grand Canyon is another U.S. landmark. People visit it to see its shapes and colors.

Parts of the **Grand Canyon** are **about 6,000 FEET** (1,800 meters) deep.

About **330 million** people live in the **United States**.

**Denali rises** more than **20,000 feet** (6,100 m) **above sea level.**

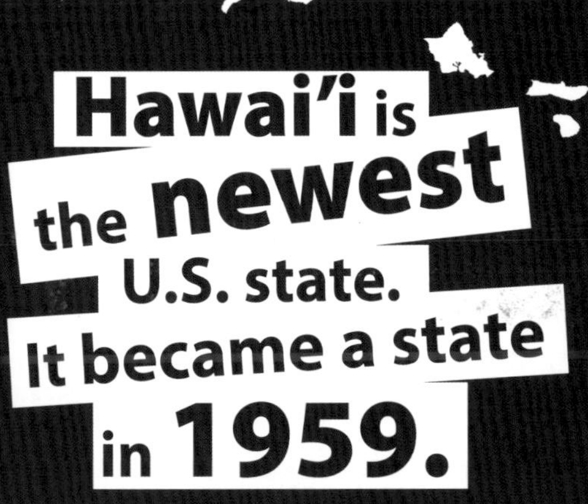

**Hawai'i** is the **newest** U.S. state. It became a state in **1959.**

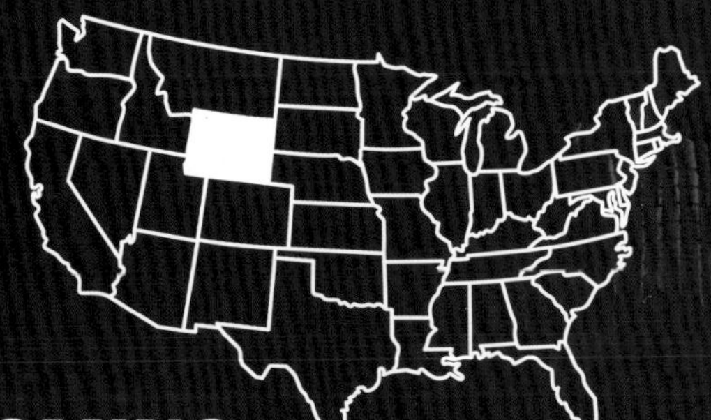

**WYOMING** is the state with the **fewest people.** About **580,000** people lived there in **2020.**

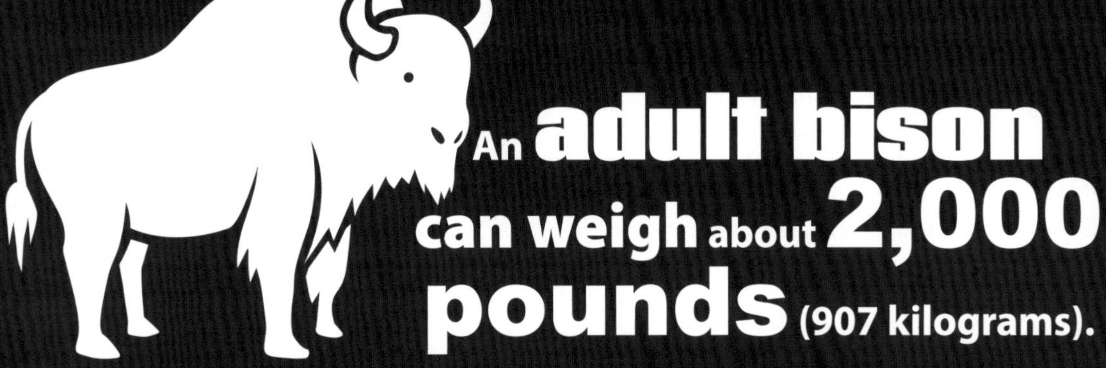

An **adult bison** can weigh about **2,000 pounds** (907 kilograms).

# KEY WORDS

Research has shown that as much as 65 percent of all written material published in English is made up of 300 words. These 300 words cannot be taught using pictures or learned by sounding them out. They must be recognized by sight. This book contains 38 common sight words to help young readers improve their reading fluency and comprehension. This book also teaches young readers several important content words, such as proper nouns. These words are paired with pictures to aid in learning and improve understanding.

| Page | Sight Words First Appearance |
|---|---|
| 4 | a, America, and, both, country, in, is, it, next, states, the, to |
| 7 | any, city, has, live, many, more, new, other, people, than |
| 8 | of, where, works |
| 11 | are, each, for, one, there |
| 13 | about, most, with |
| 16 | too |
| 18 | mountain |
| 20 | another, its, see |

| Page | Content Words First Appearance |
|---|---|
| 4 | Canada, Mexico, North America, United States |
| 7 | New York City |
| 8 | president, Washington, D.C. |
| 11 | flag, star |
| 13 | California |
| 15 | American bison, mammal, symbols |
| 16 | bald eagle, bird |
| 19 | Denali, landmarks |
| 20 | colors, Grand Canyon, shapes |

**Watch**
Video content brings each page to life.

**Browse**
Thumbnails make navigation simple.

**Read**
Follow along with text on the screen.

**Listen**
Hear each page read aloud.

Go to www.eyediscover.com and enter this book's unique code.

**BOOK CODE**

**AVF62736**